GOING PLACES

PLACES

A PLAY BY MERLE GOOD

Good Books

Intercourse, PA 17534

Design by Dawn J. Ranck
Cover design by Cheryl Benner

GOING PLACES
Copyright © 1994 by Good Books, Intercourse, PA 17534
International Standard Book Number: 1-56148-135-1
Library of Congress Card Catalog Number: 94-29236
Printed in the United States of America

Library of Congress Cataloging-in-Publication Data

Good, Merle, 1946-
    Going places : a play / by Merle Good.
        p. cm.
    ISBN 1-56148-135-1
    1. Mennonites—Drama. I. Title
PS3557.048G65   1994   94-29236
812' .54--dc20

CHARACTERS:

Susan, Mennonite farm woman, wife, mother;
    age 44 (I), 54 (II), and 64 (III).

David, Mennonite farmer, husband, father;
    age 45 (I), 55 (II).

Mervin, a son; age 24 (I), 44 (III).

Jake, a son; age 22 (I), 32 (II), and 42 (III).

Franklin, a son; age 20 (I), 30 (II), and 40 (III).

Rhoda, a daughter; age 19 (I), 29 (II), and 39 (III).

Velma, Mervin's fiancée, later his wife;
    age 21 (I), 31 (II), and 41 (III).

Jennie, Jake's girlfriend, later his wife;
    age 21 (I), 31 (II), and 41 (III).

Shirley, Franklin's wife; age 29 (II), 39 (III).

J.M., Jake and Jennie's son; age 18 (III).

Patricia, Franklin and Shirley's daughter; age 17 (III).

Joe, Mervin and Velma's son: age 19 (III).

Young J.M.; age 8 (II).

Young Patricia; age 7 (II).

Junior, Mervin and Velma's son; age 10 (III).

Anna Mary, Mervin and Velma's daughter; age 8 (III).

THE PLACE

The Zimmerman homeplace

THE TIME

Act One—August, 1969.

Act Two—March, 1979.

Act Three—October, 1989.

GOING PLACES
ACT ONE, Scene One

August, 1969. Early evening. The Zimmerman farm.

In the dark before the lights come up, traditional Mennonite a cappella voices are heard, a recording of "Take Time to Be Holy." It fills the room. Lights come up on set indicating a large farm kitchen. Susan is standing downstage right, looking out the window, intently watching something as she listens to the music. She is stirring a mixture in a large mixing bowl which she cradles in her arm as she stirs. Her eyes seem fixed, either by the music or by what she's watching. She hums along on a phrase now and then.

Jake enters upstage right and watches his mother as the music continues. He is 22, looks a bit like a student in farm clothes; he's dirty, tired, drinking a glass of meadow tea with his left hand while holding an apple in his right hand. He walks slowly up behind his mother, curious about what she's watching. She does not hear him because of the music. As the song ends, Jake bites his apple and she jumps a bit in surprise, but stays by the window.

Susan: Oh, Jake—I thought you were out with the others, helping them to unload that last wagon.

Jake: They said they were finished. *(takes another loud bite)*

Susan: Mervin and your father should be changing their clothes before these girls get back from their shopping. How come you're in here, eating the apples I need for this pie I'm trying to get into the oven?

Jake: Hey, I'll go back out and help. *(turns to go)*

Susan: No bother. They just shut off the elevator. They'll be coming in. *(turns and walks to sink area)* I worry about how hard your father works, Jake.

Jake: Oh, Mom, he's as strong as an ox. Always was.

Susan: Maybe so. Some of his sons remind me of an ox, too—only for a different reason.

Jake: That's very witty, Mom.

Susan: You and Franklin could take a lesson from your older brother.

Jake: You're not going to start that again, are you? Mervin's getting married this summer, so wouldn't you expect him to put on a good show?! Do you think he wants all of us to remember him as a lazy dunce on his last summer at home?

Susan: Mervin has never been lazy.

Jake: Yeah, what about the dunce part?

Susan: *(sighs)* Your father and I always worried that college would expand your head, Jake.

Jake: How do you mean—"expand"?

Susan: Don't act like a dunce. *(back at the window)* They're closing the barn doors.

Jake: How's it feel to have your oldest son getting married?

Susan: They make a good couple, I think. Don't you?

Jake: Yeah, probably. I just hope Velma doesn't boss Mervin around too much.

Susan: *(concerned)* Oh, Jake, what's to become of you? You always see the negative part, even in good things.

Jake: It's my job. I'm a writer.

Susan: You always say you want to be a writer—you say that being sarcastic is your job—but I don't see any paycheck.

Jake: For heaven's sake, I just graduated from college and I've lost my deferment—I'm facing the draft. And you're thinking about paychecks.

Susan: Please don't swear.

Jake: Swear? *(incredulous)* What did I say? I'm sorry if something slipped out.

Susan: You said "for heaven's sake."

Jake: That's swearing?

Susan: Someone as bright as you should be able to see that. "I swear by the heavens"—"for heaven's sake"—Grandpa Martin says it's the same thing. Don't they teach that at these Mennonite colleges?

Jake: "For heaven's sake" is swearing! You could have fooled me. That was the name of a play at the youth convention—"for heaven's sake!"

Susan: *(sadly)* So much change and worldliness these days—no one knows what's important anymore.

Jake: I know you think I'll never work as hard as Mervin does. And I know, regardless of what I do, it'll never please you as much as farming would.

Susan: I don't know how hard you can work, Jake. Your heart hasn't been in it for years.

Jake: Mom, I'm sorry that some of the things I do get you upset.

Susan: Your father has lost a lot of sleep. *(pause)* If only we had drawn the line and said you couldn't go to college.

Jake: *(mellow)* I feel the music, Mom. What can I say? I feel these things I want to express through music or writing— not just Vietnam—not just what's happening in the church with the bishops and stuff—I just FEEL things and have to express it somehow.

Susan: You've always been that way, Jake. I've never been able
            to understand it. In any case, your father and I don't
            want you to go to any more of those anti-Vietnam marches.

Jake: I don't mean it against you and Dad. I don't do it to be
            rebellious. But I have to do what I think's right.

Susan: It's not our place to stir things up.

Jake: I'm not going to lie to you, Mom. They've asked our
            group to sing at the rally in Philadelphia this weekend.

Susan: *(resigned)* With that girl, I suppose.

Jake: Don't call her that, Mom. You've met Jennie.

Susan: *(less than thrilled)* Yes, I have.

Jake: *(remembering)* Oh, she might be dropping by tomorrow
            afternoon. I meant to tell you.

Susan: Here?

Jake: No, at the end of the lane, Mom! Why do you act like she
            has the plague?

Susan: There are so many good Mennonite girls.

Jake: Yes, there are. I might even marry one some day. Right
            now I enjoy Jennie.

Susan: I don't suppose she goes to church anywhere?

Jake: Sometimes. Her parents were Quakers, she says.

Susan: They're dead?

Jake: No, they're, ahh—divorced.

Susan: *(deeply concerned)* Oh, Jake. Do you know what you're
            doing? *(pause as she turns aside)* Sometimes I worry
            that you're going to lose your soul.

Jake: *(hurt)* Lose my soul? If we Mennonites can't take a stand
            against an evil war—then we've all lost our soul!

Susan: We've always been against war—that's part of our faith.
            But this big Vietnam fuss is all politics.

Jake: Everything is political, Mom. Real people are dying.

Susan: Do you know how Grandpa Martin feels about all this?

Jake: I know your father's a bishop—so what? I can't let him
            rule my life. Besides, the bishops are losing their power
            faster than Grandpa's Plymouth runs out of gas.
            *(Franklin has entered upstage right and is listening.
            He is two years younger than Jake.)*

Franklin: And none too soon. Those guys are totally out of touch.

Susan: Franklin, you better stay out of this.

Jake: Yeah, Frankie, you better run along before you get me into
            trouble. Don't you need to change your clothes?

Franklin: I'm not the one getting married. But I must admit, I have
            smelled better. *(sniffs his armpit and makes a face)*

Jake: *(laughs, then turns serious)* Mom, I don't see why you get on my case for being against the war—when my brother here favors the war.

Susan: Jake, I think that's unfair. I don't want you to talk about your brother that way, just because you disagree.

Jake: You didn't tell her, did you, Frank? You told me you had told her.

Franklin: I said I hoped to.

Susan: Told me what?

Franklin: We can talk about it later, Jake. Tonight is Mervin and Velma's evening. I wouldn't want to spoil that.

Jake: He's not going into VS, Mom.

Susan: You're not, Franklin? Are you going to Colorado in 1-W then? *(Franklin does not respond.)*

Jake: Ask him what he thinks of communism, Mom.

Susan: Don't be foolish. We all know it's a godless evil.

Franklin: And is any Zimmerman doing anything about it?

Susan: What?

Franklin: Is there any Zimmerman in our extended family—or any Martin, for that matter—who is willing to do anything about stopping communism? *(meaningful pause)* Oh, no— our part is to say "peace, peace" when there is no peace.

Jake: You want peace, Frank—get our U.S. troops out of
            Vietnam.

Franklin: You don't get it, do you, Jake?! That Mennonite college
            is simply brainwashing you. The *communists* should get
            out of Vietnam—that's the problem. What are you
            planning to do when they come to Philadelphia—and even
            here in Lancaster County? You think you can march then?

Jake: You're joking.

Franklin: *(voice rising)* They're in Cuba, 90 miles off Florida.
            Why are you and your type so blind?

Susan: Boys, now stop it. You both scare me. I don't see why
            you can't be more obedient to the church. Now I see a car
            coming in the lane. Rhoda and Velma must be coming
            back here from their shopping. Now you fellas better
            make yourselves scarce. *(Mervin enters upstage right.*
            He's two years older than Jake, slower in movement, much
            more reserved, but wears a friendly face.)

Jake: Here's our lover boy.

Susan: Mervin, where's your father? He has to change, too. The
            girls are coming in the lane.

Mervin: He's coming.

Franklin: *(mischievous)* You know, Jake, the summer's almost
over, and we still haven't thrown this guy in the creek.
*(He makes a move on Mervin, who jumps out of his way,
and Jake joins in. Mervin is strong, but the two soon pin
him between them.)*

Jake: We got him. Think we can carry him?

Franklin: *(laughing)* I was thinking maybe we should throw Velma
into the creek first.

Jake: Great idea. Let's go grab her.

Mervin: *(loud suddenly)* You guys touch Velma and you'll be sorry.

Susan: Boys, now quit fooling around.

Mervin: You heard her.

Franklin: I see Velma coming in the walk. Shall we grab her?

Mervin: I'm warning you.

Jake: *(kidding)* I'm scared.

Franklin: I'm shaking.

Jake: Like a leaf.

Franklin: *(rolling his eyes)* Velma, Velma, Velma!

Susan: *(upset)* Now, boys, quit it. Go get cleaned up, all of you.

Jake: *(grabbing a rolling pin and throwing it at Mervin, so that he has to react quickly to catch it)* Beat you to the washbowl, lover boy. *(He exits quickly, laughing, followed by Franklin, who's chanting Velma's name, followed by Mervin, waving the rolling pin.)*

Susan: Hey, bring that rolling pin back here! *(shakes her head)* Boys, boys!!

(Lights down. Music bridges to next scene.)

ACT ONE, Scene Two

Same set. Later the same evening.

Velma Hess, Mervin's fiancée, and Rhoda, Mervin's only sister, sit at the table with lists and notes related to wedding plans, talking with excitement as Susan looks on. Mervin, clothes changed, stands across the room, properly detached.

Velma: My parents don't want any pictures taken during the wedding service, the way some are doing it these days.

Rhoda: *(a bit surprised, but knowing Velma's family is more conservative)* Well, that's okay, Mervin, isn't it?

Mervin: Whatever Velma wants.

Velma: *(laughing)* Oh, honey, I want you to be part of everything.

Mervin: Just make sure there's enough to eat at the reception!

Susan: I'm sure there will be. Landis Banquet Hall always serves lots of food. You've worked out the details with the banquet manager, I suppose. *(David enters, standing at a safe distance, observing. He is timid like his oldest son, Mervin; timid, but solid as a rock.)*

Rhoda: Oh, Mom, Velma's super organized—just look at these lists!

Mervin: You're so excited, Rhoda, if I didn't know better, I'd think you're the one who's getting married.

Rhoda: Me?! Married! No, it's just that I've never had a sister—something you boys would never understand—and now I will have one—and a good friend at that.

David: *(warmly)* Rhoda, when you were born, you were so perfect that we knew one girl was all we needed.

Rhoda: Thanks, Dad.

Velma: Oh, that's sweet. My father never says things like that.

Mervin: He's a busy man, with all his church responsibilities.

Velma: Yes, he is. And you're going to be a big relief to him, helping him on the farm.

David: I hope Mervin's up to it.

Susan: He's a good worker.

Velma: Oh, I know that. He'll make a good husband and a good father, too. *(Mervin appears uncomfortable with all the compliments.)*

(Offstage, loud humming begins in a 2-part, a cappella rendition of the wedding hymn, "Tread Softly." Everyone freezes, then turns upstage as Jake and Franklin enter, like a bride and groom walking down the aisle together, bursting into the words with great gusto):

Be silent, be silent,
A whisper is heard,
Be silent and listen,
Oh, treasure each word.
Tread softly, tread softly,
The master is here;
Tread softly, tread softly,
He bids us draw near.

(They conclude with a dramatic, harmonized flourish.)

Rhoda: *(laughing)* Nicely done.

Susan: Is this an outbreak of jealousy?

Jake: *(solemnly, to Franklin)* Do you?

Franklin: I do. *(pause, soberly)* Do you?

Jake: I do. You may now kiss the bride.

(Franklin turns formally as though to kiss his brother. Everyone is laughing. At the last minute, just before their lips meet, each raises his own hand to his lips and kisses loudly.)

Franklin: I now pronounce you—man and—and hand!

Rhoda: You guys are the works!

David: Practice may do them good.

Velma: Now I understand what Mervin meant about his brothers being wild.

Franklin: Wild? Mervin, don't tell me you've been sharing our family secrets!

Jake: *(joins in the mockery)* Velma thinks this is wild! Takes my breath away.

Mervin: *(slightly offended)* Don't mind them, Velma, they're just jealous. *(Jake and Franklin resume their formal positions and continue humming "Tread Softly." Suddenly Jake puts up his hand and they abruptly stop humming.)*

Jake: What was that? Is someone at the door?

Franklin: I'll check. You expecting someone, Mom? *(goes upstage to check)*

Susan: No.

Jake: Maybe one of our neighbors heard our music and wants to come to the wedding!

Rhoda: *(laughing)* I'm sure. *(Jennie suddenly bursts into the room, followed by Franklin. She carries a guitar and a knapsack. She is dressed like a "peace child" of the period. She rushes over to Jake and hugs him with fervor. Jake is startled, then glad to see her, then cautious about too much display of affection. It all happens so quickly that the others are frozen in place, stunned. Jennie is warm, outspokayen, at home in her body. Her ebullience brings out a defensiveness in the others in the room.)*

Jennie: *(as she rushes to him)* Jake! Oh, Jake! *(after their embrace)* You look surprised to see me.

Jake: I am. I thought you were coming tomorrow, Jennie.

Jennie: Yeah, me, too. But I got a ride up from D.C. this afternoon with George, so I tookay it. He just dropped me off.

Jake: Oh, is he outside?

Jennie: No, he's gone. *(surveying the group)* So, this is your family, Jake? *(to Susan)* He's told me so much about you guys. He loves his home so much.

Susan: He does?

Jennie: I think it's so neat, almost quaint, these days, when most of us have no home at all—to find a poet like Jake who has such a sense of roots and home.

Jake: *(trying to smooth things over)* Mother, I think you've met Jennie.

Susan: *(cautious)* Yes, I have. Hello.

Jennie: *(sweetly polite)* Hi!

Jake: And that's my sister Rhoda.

Rhoda: Hi, Jennie. Welcome.

Jennie: Thanks. Sorry if I barged in.

Jake: It's okay. This is my dad, that's my brother Franklin, and there's Mervin by the window.

Jennie: I'm pleased to meet all of you. Jake has told me so much. *(to Mervin)* Let's see, you're the farmer, right? *(He nods awkwardly.)* I think that is so—*(with a flourish)*— so avant-garde.

Franklin: *(surprised)* Farming is avant-garde?

Jennie: Oh, yes. Revolutionary, even. Wouldn't you say so, Jake? And you people are all for peace. What would the world be like, I ask you, if everyone were like you Mennonites!

Jake: *(after a pregnant pause)* And this is Velma. She and Mervin are getting married next month. He's going to help her father with his farm work.

Jennie: Congratulations.

Rhoda: Here, have a seat, Jennie. Make yourself at home.

Velma: *(standing, gathering her lists together)* Well, I think I should be getting home, if you'll take me, Mervin.

Mervin: *(relieved)* I'll be glad to. *(They move to go.)*

Susan: But I was just about to serve peach ice cream.

Mervin: Well, maybe, Mom—what do you think, Velma?

Velma: We can have ice cream another time. I should be getting home.

Mervin: Okay, see you later. *(They move abruptly upstage to go.)*

Susan: *(clearly upset by the turn of events)* You're sure we covered everything?

Jennie: I feel like I interrupted something.

Jake: It's fine, Jennie. See you guys.

David: Good night, Velma. Come again soon.

Rhoda: Bye.

Velma: *(as they go out)* Good-bye, everyone. *(Mervin nods.)*

Franklin: *(calling after them)* You two try to behave!

Susan: Franklin, why don't you help me serve the ice cream.

Jennie: *(beaming)* Sounds delicious! *(Franklin follows his mother out to the kitchen. Jake half stands, half sits.)*

David: I think I'll check that new calf in the barn. I'll be right back. *(He goes out.)*

Jake: *(calling after him)* Don't miss the ice cream, Dad.

Jennie: I feel like I scared off everybody.

Rhoda: *(less threatened than the others)* I think everyone was a little surprised, that's all.

Jake: *(laughing)* I believe you did scare Velma. She's such a prude, anyhow—it doesn't really matter.

Rhoda: She is not. That's totally unfair.

Jake: *(not wanting to argue)* Whatever you say.

Jennie: *(to Rhoda)* Let's see. Are you married?

Rhoda: Oh, no. I'm hoping to go to Africa for a year or two in church service.

Jennie: I'm against marriage, too. I tell Jake it's like slavery—and we got rid of that finally, didn't we! But it tookay a bloody war.

Rhoda: I didn't mean to say I was against marriage.

Jennie: Oh. *(pause)* Well, not everyone's had the exposure I've had—and that's cool. That's okay. Why Africa?

Rhoda: Well, I guess I'd say I care about women's issues and freedom and stuff—and I hope to go to college later—but I'm bothered how a lot of women seem more interested in privilege than in equality.

Jake: Rhoda thinks that if we men have to serve our country for a period of time, women who say they want equality should volunteer to do the same.

Jennie: You're serious?

Rhoda: Yeah, I'm not making a big thing of it. It's just the way I feel.

Jennie: But will they accept you into the army?

Rhoda: No—I want to be a peacemaker. *(Franklin enters, carrying two dishes of peach ice cream.)*

Franklin: I guess I'll serve the ladies first, if that's okay.

Jennie: Your brother's a chauvinist!

Franklin: *(clearly less than pleased)* Thanks for the compliment. I'll just set the plates on the table and you guys can fight over them. *(goes back to the kitchen)*

Jake: When it comes to food, Jennie's always first in line!

Jennie: I am not. *(jumps up and playfully pushes Jake)* You're the one who always wants to eat, especially after—*(catches herself)*

Franklin: *(re-entering)* Here, Rhoda. *(hands her a dish and then starts to eat)*

Rhoda: Thanks. *(to Jake)* You guys better quit fooling around and eat your ice cream.

Jake: *(as he catches Jennie whom he's been chasing)* I will after this young woman says she's sorry.

Susan: *(entering)* Where's your father? *(Jake quickly pulls away from Jennie.)*

Rhoda: He said he'd be right back. He went to the barn.

Jake: *(to Jennie)* Let's go out on the porch to eat. *(He exits and Jennie follows, giggling.)*

Susan: *(blunt)* Is she staying overnight?

Rhoda: *(quickly)* She can sleep in my room.

Susan: *(not very happy)* You better see that she stays there—all night. I don't want any monkey business in this house.

Rhoda: I understand.

Franklin: *(looking to see that he's not being overheard)* She's a jerk, if you ask me.

Susan: No one asked. *(starts to go back to the kitchen)* Your father wants to talk to you before he goes to bed.

Franklin: *(big sigh)* Whatever you say, Mom. *(She gives him a serious look and then goes out.)*

Rhoda: *(after they're alone)* Everyone's in trouble tonight.

Franklin: All but Rhoda—sweet Rhoda.

Rhoda: That shows how little you know, Frankie.

(Lights down. Music bridges to next scene.)

ACT ONE, Scene Three

Same set. Later the same evening.

David is standing on stage apron downstage right as a spot comes up on him. He is chewing a piece of hay, looking out across the fields from the edge of the yard. It is bedtime. The main set is dark. A second spot comes up on the stage apron downstage left. Franklin enters the spot and sees his father The conversation takes place as though they are several steps from each other

Franklin: Mother said you wanted to talk to me.

David: *(turns slightly to acknowledge his son, then back to his gaze)* I love the smell of hay this time of year.

Franklin: *(after a long pause, waiting for his dad to go on)* Yeah, me, too.

David: Reminds me of when I was a boy, raking with the horses. I still miss the horses sometimes. Tractors are great, but they make so much noise. You could hear the horses—friendly creatures—you could see them sweat, you could smell them, and smell the hay—you felt—natural—and close to the earth.

Franklin: *(chuckling)* Yeah, I bet you could really smell those horses!

David: *(reserved chuckle, smiling)* I'm sure you're right, Franklin. Young people these days don't know much about horses, do they? Unless they're rich and fancy.

Franklin: *(quickly)* I didn't mean anything by that, Dad.

David: I'm sure you didn't. *(falls silent)*

Franklin: *(after a bit)* Is that it?

David: You're in a rush?

Franklin: No.

David: You have to go some place tonight yet?

Franklin: No.

David: You have a minute, then?

Franklin: Yep.

David: *(goes back to chewing and looking at the fields)* Some decisions we make are bigger than they seem, Franklin.

Franklin: Are we talking about Voluntary Service?

David: Your mother says it sounds like you may not be going into VS.

Franklin: Probably not.

David: 1-W, then?

Franklin: I'm considering it.

David: *(slowly)* You're not contemplating running off and joining the army, are you, Franklin?

Franklin: *(knew it was coming)* I'm not sure.

David: You're not sure?

Franklin: That's what I said.

David: It seems to me that that's a question on which every young Mennonite man *should* be sure.

Franklin: And if I'm not?

David: There should be no "if's," Franklin.

Franklin: You're saying I should go into 1-W or VS, even if I'm not one hundred per cent sure that I'm a conscientious objector.

David: *(patiently)* We all have questions in life. But we can't let our questions lure us into being rash and giving up something we firmly believe in.

Franklin: You're saying it's better to be a hypocrite?

David: *(firmly)* I said no such thing. You can't go kill people, Franklin, and later say you wish you hadn't.

Franklin: Someone has to take a stand.

David: That's what I like to hear.

Franklin: No, I meant—against communism.

David: Franklin, I know you like to be independent. But you're taking this too far.

Franklin: You want me to be a CO, even if I don't believe it.

David: I want you to believe it.

Franklin: Maybe I can't.

David: *(after a long pause)* You'll break your mother's heart, you know that.

Franklin: I have to be true to myself.

David: *(voice concerned and partly angry)* You should want to be true to God.

Franklin: You think all the thousands in the armed forces don't believe in God?!

David: Franklin, you know what I'm saying. *(very firm)* I forbid you to join the military.

Franklin: And if I do? *(David does not answer.)* Talk about hypocrites—my brother encourages the war by encouraging the godless communists. He marches—and he sings—and he fools around with that hippie Jennie.

David: *(warning)* Careful.

Franklin: But I'm not sarcastic and cynical—I'm sincere. I really think what we have in this country didn't just happen— people paid a price for it. And I'm willing to pay a price, too. What's wrong with that?

David: *(angry)* Well, then, Franklin, while you're computing the price, you better know that this is such a weighty matter to your mother and me—that there is a very good chance—if you go off to the war—things may not be the same between us.

Franklin: Whoa! Are you threatening to disinherit me if I join the army?!

David: That could be part of the price you're aching to pay. You'll lose your membership in the church, too.

Franklin: *(livid)* You just made my decision for me, Dad. You're trying to bribe me into being a hypocrite.

David: You're getting me all wrong. Don't twist things, Franklin.

Franklin: No, I'm getting you right. You're threatening to cut me off from this family financially if I don't do what you want! What ever happened to love?!

David: Love is what it's all about, Franklin. "Love your enemies. Do not kill."

Franklin: How about "love your children"?

David: *(still angry, but stung by the question)* Franklin, I do love you. Very much.

Franklin: You have a funny way of showing it. *(angry)* I can't believe this family. *(He turns to storm out, then spins back to his father, his anger mixed with injury.)* What about Jake? Why do you look the other way with him? *(He storms out.)*

David: *(calling after him)* Franklin! Don't do anything rash, Franklin. *(He turns slowly back to the fields, his face full of concern and worry.)*

(Lights down. Intermission.)

ACT TWO, Scene One

Ten years later. March, 1979. Friday afternoon. The set has undergone minor changes to signal the movement of time.

Rhoda is seated at the table, sorting slides. As the lights come up, Susan enters, carrying a freshly baked cake.

Susan: So this is where you disappeared to, Rhoda.

Rhoda: Yeah, I'm trying to get these slides organized for tonight. Besides, I can't quilt as well as you and Velma. Is that the birthday cake?

Susan: Isn't it a beauty! You can help to decorate it later, after it cools, if you wish.

Rhoda: I'd love to, Mother, if I have time.

Susan: Remember, Velma and Mervin are going to show a few slides, too, from their trip to Central America. *(turns to go back to the kitchen)*

Rhoda: I'm only doing this because Dad asked me to. I'm not one to trot around to churches with my "missionary slide show."

Susan: *(pausing, cake still in hand)* Meaning what?

Rhoda: *(clearly trying to make sure Velma cant hear her in the front room)* Is it me, or is Velma more difficult than she used to be?

Susan: Rhoda, you've only been home from Africa for a month, remember that.

Rhoda: It's just that she's so bossy. She used to be my best friend, and now she treats me like I'm her not-so-smart daughter or something.

Susan: *(carefully)* I guess, because you aren't married, she can't help but think of you as "one of the girls."

Rhoda: I find it offensive that people treat me like less of a person just because I'm single.

Susan: *(coming back toward the table, lowering her voice)* You think of yourself as single—she thinks you as an "old maid"—an old maid, I might add, who's planning to go to seminary, an idea which Velma finds very offensive. So I guess it's not hard to see why the two of you aren't best friends anymore.

Rhoda: She's gotten so conservative.

Susan: And you've gotten so liberal, like so many who go into MCC.

Rhoda: I don't want to argue about MCC, or being single, or going to seminary, Mother. It's Dad's birthday, and I was only organizing some slides because he asked for it.

Susan: I want to see the slides, too.

Rhoda: *(a bit irritated)* I spent six years in Africa over the past ten years, and wouldn't you know Mervin and Velma flutter around Central America for nine days on a deputation for their little mission committee—and they come back talking like experts.

Velma: *(offstage, calling)* Mom!

Susan: I hope she didn't hear you.

Rhoda: I don't care if she did.

Velma: *(offstage, closer)* Mom! *(enters)* Oh, here you are. Am I supposed to finish the quilt by myself?

Susan: I'll be right there.

Velma: Okay, Mom. If we're going to have that quilt ready for the relief sale next Saturday, we better keep it moving.

Susan: *(moving toward kitchen)* I'm coming, Velma. *(exits to kitchen)*

Velma: You're still sorting your slides, Rhoda?! Mervin organized his as soon as we got home.

Rhoda: I'm sure he did.

Velma: It's such a good way to help people back here to see the spiritual need, wouldn't you say?

Rhoda: I suppose so.

Velma: You mean, maybe you didn't see the spiritual needs in Africa?

Rhoda: Velma, you know it's more complicated than that.

Velma: Mervin said in his sermon Sunday that faith is such a simple thing. You either believe or you don't.

Rhoda: You can't export your own culture into another country and think it's mission. That's imperialistic and paternalistic.

Velma: Well, I don't know about all your "listics." I do know Jesus didn't say anything about "exports," but he sure did tell us to go into all the world, to every nation, and to share the good news of his love.

Susan: *(re-entering)* Okay, Velma, shall we head back to the quilting?

Velma: And he didn't say anything about women going against the natural order and trying to be preachers.

Susan: Oh, look who comes here.

Rhoda: I don't want to argue, Velma.

Susan: *(as Young J.M. enters)* Good afternoon, J.M. How was school? *(Young J.M. is eight years old. He is dressed in informal spring school clothes.)*

Y.J.M.:   Hello, Grandma. It was okay, I guess.

Rhoda: Hello, J.M.

Y.J.M.:   Hi, Aunt Rhoda. Oh, hello, Aunt Velma.

Velma: Hello, J.M. Well, I'm going back to the front room to continue quilting, and I hope I won't be alone. *(exits)*

Susan: *(to Young J.M.)* Can I get you a snack?

Y.J.M.: Maybe later. I want to go ride my bike and see what Grandpa's doing out in the steer barn.

Susan: Okay, I'll help Velma with the quilt then. Let me know when you want your snack. I put your other jacket up in your room with your suitcase.

Y.J.M.: Thanks, Grandma. *(He exits upstairs with his backpack and jacket.)*

Rhoda: Does he often stay here overnight?

Susan: Oh, some weeks not at all, some weeks as many as three nights—ever since Jake and Jennie were separated. *(She moves to go back to quilting.)*

Rhoda: You think they'll go through with the divorce? *(Susan is a strong woman, but she clearly has her breath taken away by the question. For a moment she appears about to crumble under the strain, ever so imperceptibly.)*

Susan: I hope not. *(Her voice has changed to a mellow-hush, with a touch of quiver)* I pray every morning and every night that they will find a way to be reconciled.

Rhoda: *(without moving)* I'm sorry, Mother, I didn't mean to upset you. I know it's hard.

Susan: Nothing in my whole life has been so hard, Rhoda. I'm not quite sure why. This family's been through a lot. Jake and his peacenik days. Mervin and Velma leaving our church and going with the conservative split. You going off to Africa. Jake and Jennie living together without being married. Oh, my, sometimes I asked God why he had chosen us for this—endless trial. *(She pauses, trying to keep her composure.)* But even your father's illness—as scary and painful as it is—and I don't know why—but even the accident itself last year—as terrible as it was—when Jake and Jennie lost little Annie in that—that horrible crash—*(a loud sob slips out, beyond her control)*—even that—was not as hard as seeing the two of them getting divorced. *(Rhoda gets up and crosses to her mother, reaching out her arms. They embrace in a restrained sort of way.)*

Rhoda: I'm so sorry, Mother.

Susan: *(still embracing)* I don't quite understand it. I've never cried so much.

Rhoda: It's okay to cry, Mother.

Susan: *(pulling away)* I suppose. But I wish things were different. *(She blows her nose, wipes her tears, and goes toward the kitchen. Young J.M. re-enters from upstairs in play clothes and a different jacket. He clears his throat to signal his presence. Susan exits to kitchen without lookaying back. Young J.M. seems to take emotional scenes in stride. He walks over to look at Rhoda's slides as she sits down at the table again.)*

Rhoda: Oh, hi, J.M. Heading out to ride your bike?

Y.J.M.: Yeah. You know, you should come and ride with me, Aunt Rhoda. I've hardly seen you since you're home from Africa.

Rhoda: Maybe later. Right not I gotta finish these slides for Grandpa's birthday party tonight.

Y.J.M.: You going to show us pictures of elephants?

Rhoda: Uh—no—I don't think I have any pictures of elephants. Sorry.

Y.J.M.: I like elephants.

Rhoda: Yeah, me, too.

Y.J.M.: I thought there were a lot of elephants in Africa.

Rhoda: Oh, there are. I just don't have any pictures of any.

Y.J.M.: I'm disappointed.

Rhoda: Well, I'm sorry you're disappointed. *(a touch testy)* You'll probably get over it if you go ride your bike.

Y.J.M.: Elephants are my favorite animals. Always have been.

Rhoda: It certainly sounds that way.

Y.J.M.: If I ever go to Africa, I'm taking a hundred pictures of elephants. *(He turns to go.)*

Rhoda: See you later.

Y.J.M.: All these years you've been in Africa, Aunt Rhoda, every time Grandma and I prayed for you, I always figured you were friends with the elephants.

Rhoda: *(trying to be cordial)* Bye, bye, J.M. *(He turns and exits outdoors. Rhoda goes back to her slides.)*

Velma: *(entering)* I'm still the only person in the front room quilting.

Rhoda: Oh, I'm sorry, Velma. Mother—got delayed. I'm sure she's coming.

Velma: *(silent for a moment, watching her sort slides)* You have any pictures of elephants?

Rhoda: *(trying to restrain herself)* No, I don't have any pictures of elephants.

Velma: How can you have slides from Africa and not have any elephants?!

Rhoda: *(raising her voice in exasperation)* Why's everyone so interested in elephants? I didn't go to Africa to work with *elephants*. I went to try to help *people*.

Velma: What's your problem, Rhoda? You don't have to get mad. Look, please tell Mom I can use her help.

Rhoda: Sorry. I'll send her in as soon as she shows up.

Velma: *(cheerfully)* Thanks. *(goes to exit)* All I can say is if Mervin went to Africa, you can be sure he'd have plenty of slides of elephants. But that just goes to show the difference between men and women—a subject with which I recognize that you're not very familiar. *(Rhoda is ready to retort when the phone rings. She gets up to answer it, but Susan re-enters and gets there first.)*

Susan: Hello. Oh, hi, Mervin. Yeah, she's standing right here. *(gestures to Velma)* It's for you.

Velma: *(going to phone)* What does he want? *(in phone)* Hello, Mervin. What's up? *(pause)* What? You're kidding. When? Well, where did they go? Is it serious? You're sure? No, I can leave. I always told you that that Jonathan wasn't too smart. Okay, bye now. *(She hangs up.)*

Susan: Trouble?

Velma: Our hired man Jonathan just left in the middle of the afternoon.

Rhoda: Was he upset?

Velma: Mervin said it has something to do with an accident at Three Mile Island.

Susan: Oh, I heard something on the radio this morning. It didn't make it sound too serious.

Velma: Well, apparently the television people are trying to stir things up. Mervin says Jonathan's wife came with their two small children to our place and insisted that he go along to her home in northern Pennsylvania to get away from TMI.

Rhoda: That sounds pretty bad.

Velma: I'm sure it's overblown. You can see the towers from our farm, and our neighbor man works there. Mervin said he called that man's wife, and she said she hasn't heard anything. So it's just that some folks panic at the smallest thing, I guess. In any case, it sounds like I better head home to help with the chores.

Susan: The quilt can wait.

Velma: Well, I guess I better get my things and be off. *(She exits toward front room.)*

Rhoda: I've always been concerned that one of those nuclear power plants will blow up one of these days.

Susan: Oh, don't talk foolish, Rhoda. *(looks out)* Well, who's that coming in the lane? It looks like Jennie's car.

Rhoda: Were you expecting her?

Susan: No. I can't imagine why she's coming. *(brightly)* Maybe it's good news.

Rhoda: Maybe she's coming for J.M.

Susan: I doubt it. *(Velma re-enters)* This is Jake's turn to take
           care of him.

Velma: I pity that child. He needs both love and discipline.

Susan: Careful what you say, Velma. *(goes toward door)* Well,
           this is a surprise. Come in, Jennie. *(Jennie enters)*

Jennie: *(with no niceties)* Did Jake call?

Susan: This afternoon? I don't think so. *(looks at Rhoda)*

Rhoda: Not that I know of.

Jennie: He can be such a jerk.

Susan: Is something wrong?

Jennie: Is something wrong! We're about to have a nuclear
           holocaust and you ask if something's wrong! Where's J.M.?

Susan: Out riding his bike or visiting with Grandpa.

Jennie: We're leaving. I'm taking him with me.

Rhoda: Are you talking about Three Mile Island?

Velma: Mervin says it's nothing serious.

Jennie: I suppose Mervin would. You think the governor's lying?

Susan: What?

Jennie: You don't have the radio on? Oh, I forgot, Mervin
           doesn't approve. The governor held a press conference
           and urged all pregnant women and all young children
           to leave the area.

Susan: He did? When?

Jennie: Several hours ago. I've been trying to reach Jake at the
           newspaper building—and I finally talked to that reporter
           he often works with—Lucy—and she said that he's *at*
           TMI, covering the accident.

Rhoda: How bad is it?

Jennie: They're saying that if the core melts down, it will release
           deadly nuclear material into the air and it could kill
           everyone who breathes the air.

Susan: And Jake's at TMI? I wonder if he knows how bad it is.

Velma: It's easy to exaggerate.

Jennie: You of all people, Velma, should be evacuating. Where
           are your children?

Velma: At home.

Jennie: You don't care if they get leukemia—or worse?

Velma: Mervin says it's fine.

Jennie: How does he know?

Velma: Our neighbor works there.

Jennie: And you're sure your neighbor hasn't been killed in the
           accident? The whole thing's top secret. There's no way
           we know what's happening. Clearly the governor is very,
           very concerned. *(For a moment, they all fall silent.)* Well,
           I'm taking J.M. and leaving. If Jake calls, tell him we're

heading for the Jersey shore to get as far away as we can.
I'll try to reach him through his office. *(suddenly mad)* I
think it is outrageous that he couldn't take the time to call
and warn us! His own family.

Susan: I'll get J.M.'s suitcase. *(goes upstairs)*

Jennie: I'm going out to find him. *(pauses before going out)*
Velma, I know we're as different as night and day, but I
think you should think of your children first this time.

Velma: We'll be careful, Jennie. But we do have cows to milk.
We can't just run off to New Jersey.

Jennie: This is not a trivial thing. Millions could die.

Velma: We better all pray that they don't. *(Susan re-enters with
suitcase and jacket. She hurries over to Jennie.)*

Susan: I think this is everything.

Jennie: Thanks.

Susan: Be careful.

Jennie: I will. Be sure to let Jake know how upset I was.

Susan: I hope he's okay.

Jennie: He's crazy to be there, that's all I can say. Anything to be
a famous writer. See you. *(She hurries out.)*

Velma: She hasn't changed a bit.

Susan: I guess most of us haven't. Rhoda, I'm going out to tell
your father what's happening.

Velma: I'm on my way, too. *(She crosses to exit.)* I'll call you later, Mom. See you, Rhoda.

Rhoda: Yeah, see you. *(Velma exits.)* Mom, can I help with something?

Susan: Just stay by the phone, in case Jake calls. And now that Velma's gone, I guess we can turn the radio on.

Rhoda: I wish I knew how bad it is.

Susan: *(nodding)* I'll be back in a few minutes. *(Susan goes out. Rhoda walks downstage to watch the comings and goings outside.)*

Rhoda: So much for Dad's birthday party.

(Lights down as music bridges to next scene.)

ACT TWO, Scene Two

Same set. Later the same day.

Franklin, now 30, and David, now 55, are both standing downstage, looking out at the fields, presumably through windows of the house. David wears a modest dress shirt and pants and a cardigan sweater. Franklin wears a suit and tie and appears to be well-to-do, although the outfit has a bit of a cheap feel to it.

David: The radio makes it sound pretty serious, Franklin.

Franklin: Yeah, it does. But I'm not so sure, Dad. Maybe one should be a little skeptical of the media these days.

David: I see.

Franklin: I called Donald Burkholder who works at the Christian Broadcasting station, you know, and he told me there's no proof of anything. In fact, he said he wouldn't be surprised that it's all being staged to create a scare against the nuclear industry.

David: I hope it doesn't hurt the land.

Franklin: Oh, I don't really think there's anything to worry about. As a realtor, I should be the first one to be concerned— but I honestly think it's just a big scare.

David: I hope you're right. I wish Jake would call.

Franklin: Oh, I'll bet he's eating this up! He always likes the sensational stuff.

David: I'd rather if you didn't criticize your brother, Franklin.

Franklin: I'm sorry if I sounded that way, Dad. I don't mean to be unfair. But you gotta admit it's rather surprising the way he and his newspaper can ignore the really major issues facing our society—but anything related to nuclear power gets them going. *(Franklin's wife Shirley has entered during this speech. She is pretty, dressed also in a would-be big-time look, and moves like a self-assured but cheap Barbie doll.)*

Shirley: *(voice has an affected purr)* Oh, honey, don't be criticizing your brother. His life hasn't been easy, you know. *(The men turn and move to other parts of the room, as though to make space for her.)*

Franklin: As though mine has.

Shirley: It is funny, though, I agree, how some people go bananas over anything nuclear—and not a soul has died in years and years—though it sure scares those communists! But those same people don't care about the thousands—millions, even—who are murdered every year at these abortion clinics. It's a holocaust right under our noses—and those liberals in Washington and right here in Lancaster County couldn't care one iota.

Franklin: You're right about that, Shirley.

Shirley: I tell you, Daddy, you have no idea how callous and hard-hearted some of these people can be. It's a sin. I had a customer just this afternoon in my bookstore who shared with me the latest statistics on this horrible tragedy. It boggles my mind. *(David simply nods; he seems a bit unsure how to handle Shirley.)*

Franklin: So it's almost comical to see a little accident at a nuclear power plant have all these liberals peeing in their pants.

Shirley: Oh, watch your language, Franklin dear.

Franklin: I'm just trying to let Dad know it's nothing to worry about.

Shirley: Oh, I understand why you're concerned, Daddy. My parents called from Colorado, all upset. They'd heard it on the news. I can see they'd be worried. *(pause)* I just pray that someday soon they'll come to know the Lord, as we do.

David: *(pause)* I worry a little about Mervin and Velma and their children, living right there on top of TMI.

Shirley: They are close enough, that's for sure. Too bad they can't come to the party tonight. I can't believe their hired man just up and ran away like that.

Franklin: *(a bit critical)* Yeah, and if Jennie hadn't panicked and run off with J.M., he could be here to play with Trisha.

David: Where is my little Patricia anyhow?

Shirley: She's upstairs with her Aunt Rhoda, looking at something about Africa.

David: *(poignant)* They grow up so fast, don't they?

Franklin: Yes, they do. *(awkward pause)* Did the—the doctor— have anything new to say?

David: No, ah—well, no, I guess not—I mean, he talks a lot, you know—but it seems things aren't responding like he thought they might.

Franklin: I'm sorry, Dad.

Shirley: Yeah, me, too. Is there anything at all we can do for you, Daddy?

David: Thanks for asking. People have been so helpful, so wonderful. Even some of our neighbors—some who were, ah—a bit hard to get to know—some of them dropped by, or sent a card or some food. *(His voice swells with emotion, but he maintains control.)* It's been amazing to me, really, how much—how much love there is all around us.

Shirley: *(mellow)* We pray for you every day, Daddy.

David: I know you do. I appreciate it. I guess we'll just continue with the chemotherapy.

Franklin: God will bring you through, Dad. I know that awful bout with pneumonia I had two years ago really brought me closer to the Lord.

David: *(quoting)* "And from his fullness have we all received grace upon grace." *(Franklin nods.)*

Y.Patric: *(calling from offstage)* Grandpa! Mommy! Daddy!

Shirley: We're in here, Trisha honey.

Y.Patric: I know. Are you ready?

Shirley: She wants us all to sit down so she can do a little show for us.

David: *(finding a seat)* Okay. *(calling)* Mother, you don't want to miss this. *(Susan enters from kitchen with apron on and sits as Young Patricia, age 7, parades in, costumed in African clothes, looking and walking like a princess. Rhoda follows, all smiles.)*

Franklin: Oh, looky here!

Susan: You look very impressive, Patricia.

Shirley: Is that our little girl?!

Y.Patric: *(pausing center stage and pretending to curtsy)* Hello! *(She spins in a circle.)*

Franklin: She even speaks Swahili!

Y.Patric: Hello! *(They all laugh. At that moment, Jake, now 32, enters. At first they don't see him. But Rhoda does.)*

Rhoda: Jake! Where'd you come from? *(Suddenly they are all on their feet. Young Patricia, seeing that she's lost her audience and hearing the urgency in the voices, slips off to a corner to play with dolls.)*

Susan: We thought you were at TMI.

Jake: I was. *(Everyone is still, waiting. He is visibly shaken.)* Things are crazy.

Rhoda: What do you mean?

Jake: Well, I don't want to scare you but a meltdown is still possible.

Susan: You mean it's not under control yet?

Jake: Nobody knows anything for sure, it seems.

Franklin: *(coaxing)* Oh, Jake, you were always one to exaggerate.

Jake: *(ignores him)* What is so unnerving is seeing the bigwigs, who are supposed to know everything—they are clearly scared—they were scurrying around and they refused to talk to us.

Franklin: Maybe they had problems to solve. That hardly signals the end of the world.

Jake: *(sidestepping the bait)* I sincerely hope you're right, Frankie. Where's J.M.?

David: Oh, you didn't know?

Susan: Jennie was hoping you would call.

Jake: Jennie?

Rhoda: She said she left a message for you at your office.

Jake: Could be. I haven't been back to the newspaper building yet. Phones are tied up. I was on my way home to shower and change clothes—and maybe catch a few winks before heading back to TMI for the night.

Susan: But why must you go back?

Jake: I'm a reporter, remember? But where's J.M.?

Rhoda: *(carefully)* Jennie took him—after the governor called for an evacuation.

Jake: He's not under three years old! Don't tell me she's overreacting again. I'm going to call her.

Susan: No, they left the area.

Shirley: They went to New Jersey.

Jake: New Jersey?

Shirley: To get away.

Franklin: Chickens coming home to roost.

Jake: *(turning abruptly, clearly irritated)* What exactly does that mean, Frank?

Franklin: It's what happens when you reporters scare people with—with unsubstantiated stories. People run. Even your own—*(searching for precise term)*—wife.

Jake: Just watch what you say, buddy. I haven't had a lot of sleep. We have a real crisis here, whether you believe it or not.

Franklin: Hey, Jake, I'm sorry. I know you're under a lot of stress. And even though I disagree about how serious it is, I didn't mean to upset you.

Susan: Jennie said she'll call when they stop for the night. I'm sure she'll call.

David: I'm worried about Mervin and his family.

Jake: *(shakes his head)* Yeah, I stopped there when I left TMI on my way here. They act unconcerned. Of course, what options do they have? They can't just leave and take their herd of cows along.

Susan: But it *is* a real crisis, isn't it?

Jake: Yes, it definitely is. If you saw the number of government vehicles which have arrived from Washington—and the helicopters—there's no doubt there's a crisis.

Franklin: It mustn't be too bad if you're thinking of heading back there, Jake. You were never one to risk your own hide! *(catches himself)* I didn't mean that the way it came out. What I meant was—

Jake: Maybe you should talk less and think a little more, Big-Shot Realtor. *(The phone rings and Rhoda goes to answer.)*

Rhoda: Hello. Oh, Jennie. Just a minute. *(to Jake)* It's Jennie.

Franklin: Maybe we should be heading home, Shirley.

Jake: Better finalize some of those real estate deals before the land values drop!

Franklin: Putting me down doesn't prove you're right, brother.

Susan: Patricia, could you come to the kitchen to help me for a minute?

Y.Patric: Sure, Grandma. *(She follows Susan to the kitchen. Shirley appears to follow, but pauses at the doorway to listen to Jake on the phone. Franklin glares at his brother, then walks away from the phone as Jake goes to answer. Everyone is listening to Jake on the phone.)*

Jake: Where are you, Jennie? *(pause)* No, I wasn't snapping at you, I just want to know where you are. Valley Forge? That's not in New Jersey. No, I'm not insulting anyone, Jennie. For heaven's sake, is J.M. alright? He is? May I talk to him? No, I want to right now. *(He glances around at the others and the room, seems a bit sheepish about his word tangle with Jennie, but seems too tired to get ahead of things.)* Hi, J.M. Are you okay? Yes, I am. No, I'm okay, I really am. Okay, well, do what your mom says. Okay, good night. I love you, too. *(pause)* Jennie, are you okay? You have enough money? Okay, what's the phone number there? Uh-huh. *(writes it down)* Right. Okay, I'll try to call you because I have no idea where I'll be. What? Oh, I will. What? Oh, thanks, Jennie. I'll be careful. Bye. (*He hangs up. There is silence for a moment. Then he speaks to the others in the room.*) They're fine. They're at a motel in Valley Forge. *(pause)* Jennie's been really jumpy—ever since we lost—ah—*(He can't finish the sentence.)*

Rhoda: Oh, that's understandable. (*Suddenly Young Patricia enters, carrying the birthday cake with candles burning. Susan is right behind her, and she begins the song, "Happy Birthday." Everyone joins in. Young Patricia carries the cake toward the table. Everyone is smiling as the song ends.*)

Y.Patric: Can you blow them all out in one breath, Grandpa?

David: *(laughing)* I'll try. (*He blows hard, but it takes a second breath to get them all.*)

Franklin: Happy birthday, Dad.

Rhoda: Yeah, happy birthday.

Shirley: In spite of everything.

Jake: I almost forgot.

Susan: Happy birthday, "Grandpa."

Y.Patric: Wait! Wait, everyone! Make a wish. Make a wish, Grandpa.

David: *(pauses, then blurts it out, not in criticism, but in pure hopefulness)* I hope God lets me live long enough to see peace come to our family. *(For a fleeting second, everyone is frozen. Then the lights comes down to end the scene.)*

(Lights down. Music bridges to next scene.)

ACT TWO, Scene Three

Same set. Later the same evening.

Jake is standing on stage apron downstage right as a spot comes up on him. He appears motionless, staring into the twilight. The main set is dark. A second spot comes up on the stage apron downstage left. David enters the spot, then sees his son. The conversation takes place as though they are several steps from each other David wears the same clothes, Jake a new shirt and a different jacket. Jake turns as David arrives, then turns back to the twilight.

David: *(after a moment)* Mother said she thought that looked like your car out by the barn.

Jake: Sorry, I didn't mean to bother you.

David: No problem.

Jake: I've always loved the twilight. It seems full of tenderness—and promises.

David: I know what you mean. *(pause)* Maybe I'm intruding.

Jake: No. I couldn't sleep. So I took my shower and I'm on my way back to the Island. But I wanted to see the home-place one last time.

David: Jake, I wonder if you couldn't just call in and say you can't come.

Jake: You think I should? *(David doesn't answer)* People like
          to make fun of reporters—and I agree, a lot of what we
          do is humdrum—but at times like this the public counts
          on us to bring them life-and-death information.

David: You've always been dedicated to your writing, Jake—I
          can't fault you on that. *(pause)* You think a lot of us will
          die?

Jake: I don't know. I look into the twilight tonight, and I don't
          know what to think. Has the damage already been done—
          has the nuclear poison been accidently released into the
          atmosphere—will we all start to die soon—will the land
          be contaminated and the crops wither and disappear?
          Or—has no damage been done—the danger is real—but
          no damage to anyone's health? Which is it? Will we be
          told? Will we ever find out—before the children start to
          die?

David: It would be a terrible thing if the land were destroyed.

Jake: What am I?—the ninth generation on this same farm—
          some of the best soil in the whole world in those fields
          out there. And this modern menace is capable of
          contaminating everything.

David: You almost sound like you wish you were a farmer, Jake.

Jake: I love the land, that I do.

David: But you don't want to farm it. *(Jake looks at him, but
          does not answer He turns back to the fields.)*

Jake: Funny thing, one of the students I have in that writing course I teach—she grew up in Nevada. And when she was young, her parents learned about those nuclear tests out there in the desert—so they decided to move away and they looked for a safe place to go to—they chose "the garden spot of America"—they moved here to Lancaster County! Now Nevada sounds safer.

David: Well, we certainly should pray.

Jake: I suppose so.

David: You sound unconvinced.

Jake: *(carefully)* You know, Dad, that faith and piety have never been my strong suit.

David: You don't think God is in control of a situation like this?

Jake: I gave up any hope of God being in control when we lost our little Annie in that accident.

David: I'm sorry. I didn't mean to be insensitive.

Jake: God didn't build those nuclear towers—people did. And if those towers are out of control, it's not God's fault—it's simply a matter of human beings losing control of what they built.

David: But that doesn't mean we can't pray.

Jake: *(after a pause)* Well, I better get going. *(carefully)* Mother says the doctor wants you to go back for treatments.

David: Yes. It doesn't sound too good.

Jake: Well, I'm sorry, Dad.

David: Thanks.

Jake: You really need help here on the farm.

David: It looks like the Stauffer boy can help.

Jake: You mean Menno Stauffer's boy?

David: Yeah, the second one—his name is Norman.

Jake: They went with the conservative split, didn't they?

David: Yes, they did. But they're a good family.

Jake: Well, Dad—I hope—and pray—that your health will be restored.

David: They can do a lot with cancer these days.

Jake: Yes, they can.

David: You know, Jake, I don't want to upset you by saying this. I want to live—and I hope God spares me. But if he doesn't, I've made my peace. I want my children to know that. I've had a good life.

Jake: That's terrible to talk like that, Dad. You've got to fight this thing.

David: Oh, I'm fighting. Very hard. But I guess I'm even more concerned about you, Jake—you and Jennie—than I am about myself. *(Jake looks at his father uncertainly, not with resentment or anger, but unsure how to respond.)*

Jake: *(after a pause)* I better be going.

David: I hope I didn't upset you.

Jake: No—ah—I, ah—I wish I could explain it.

David: *(blurts it out)* You're not divorced yet. You could always turn around and patch it up, couldn't you? *(Jake doesn't answer)* I'm sorry. I shouldn't have said that. It's hard for your mother and me to just stand by. We feel so—helpless.

Jake: Well, I gotta go. *(He moves as though to go, then pauses.)* I'll probably regret saying this, but it does feel like we're standing on the rim of the earth tonight. Jennie never wanted a second child, Dad. She wanted to have an abortion. And I fought her on it. I know most of the family thinks I'm liberal on everything, and I do support a woman's right to choose—but this was my baby, too. I pled with Jennie to have the child—we argued and argued, every day for weeks—and she finally gave in. She agreed to have the baby. *(pause)* And when little Annie was born, she was so wonderful—she captured Jennie's heart—I don't know how else to say it—well, you saw it—that baby "captured" Jennie's whole being—and then we argued again—all the time. I loved Annie, too—but I thought Jennie was spoiling her—she gave her everything she wanted. We argued and argued. And then—so suddenly—the accident—I was driving, of course. To say Jennie's heart was broken is understating it—I think she felt like her heart was ripped from her body. *(Jake fights to keep composure.)* Well, so did I. We both suffered so much—but we didn't argue a word. Not one time. Silence came between us. But I can see it in her eyes—the blame, the pain, the rage—but I can't reach her. It's as though we have lost everything, Dad—we can't find common ground for our grief—we can't forgive—we can't let go—we can't make peace. *(Jake turns away from his father, wiping his tears.)*

David: *(deeply moved, but still composed)* I'm sorry, Jake. I had no idea.

Jake: I know you didn't. *(long pause as he regains his composure)* Well, I really must go. The twilight's gone. *(pause)* Maybe you shouldn't tell Mother about this.

David: It might help her understand.

Jake: Well, I'll leave it to you. Good night, Dad. *(He exits away from his father)*

David: Good night, son. Do be careful. *(He looks after him. When he is alone, his hand comes up to his strong face, and we can see that David is fighting tears, his face filled with anguish. His words are more of a cry than a prayer)* Dear God!

(Lights down. Audience lights up slowly. Intermission.)

ACT THREE, Scene One

Ten years later. October, 1989. Sunday afternoon. The set has undergone minor changes to signal the movement of time.

J.M. is seated on an upholstered chair, right of center, looking at a photo album as the lights come up. He is now 18, dressed in a coat and tie, with a collegiate look. Patricia enters upstage right, carrying a pie. She is dressed in jeans, an informal shirt, and a casual jacket. She is 17, a bit younger than her cousin.

Patricia: Oh, hi, J.M. *(She pauses halfway to the kitchen, pie in hand.)*

J.M.: Hi there, Trisha. How's my favorite cousin?

Patricia: Where is everyone?

J.M.: Oh, they went for a walk. Grandma said it was such a nice afternoon that she wanted to take a walk. You missed a great Sunday dinner, Trisha.

Patricia: Yeah, I know. I had to work at the restaurant.

J.M.: The pie's your peace offering?

Patricia: I guess you could say that, J.M. I know Grandma doesn't like that I work on Sundays. Well, my parents don't either. But Dad insisted I get a job so I "learn how to work!" You'd think we're rich enough. I snitched a pie at the restaurant for Grandma—which was sorta dumb, now that I think about it. Her pies are better than this one. *(goes to the kitchen)*

J.M.: It's the thought that counts, Trisha.

Patricia: *(re-entering)* So you didn't go along on the walk?

J.M.: No, it's not my kind of thing.

Patricia: What are you looking at?

J.M.: An old photo album.

Patricia: *(looking over his shoulder)* Let me see. Oh, who's that—is that you, J.M.? *(laughs)* Look at you!— that's me in Grandpa's lap. Look at my crazy expression.

J.M.: Grandpa looks pleased enough.

Patricia: Yeah, he does. *(with feeling)* I really miss him.

J.M.: Here, you can have the album, Trisha. I looked at most of it.

Patricia: Thanks. *(She takes it and pulls out a chair from the table, turning it so she faces J.M. as she pages through the album.)* How do you like Philadelphia?

J.M.: Okay, I guess. I haven't been around the city that much, but the part near the university is nice enough.

Patricia: You like college?

J.M.:   Oh, yeah. It's tough at these Ivy League schools, but I enjoy the challenge. I'm hoping to go right on into the Wharton School, of course, to do my MBA.

Patricia: Oh, that's great. I'm really impressed. *(pause)* Oh, look at this picture of our dads on a fishing boat!

J.M.:   *(stretches to see)* That must have been that famous deep-sea fishing trip. They really look like brothers there.

Patricia: Yeah. Dad says you dropped by his office yesterday.

J.M.:   Yeah, I'd like to help Uncle Franklin in his campaign.

Patricia: *(surprised)* Really, J.M.?

J.M.:   Yeah, if he'll have me.

Patricia: Why would you want to work in a little insignificant race for commissioner? There must be something better to do in Philadelphia than come back here on weekends to help Dad.

J.M.:   Your dad's a strong candidate.

Patricia: He's already run and lost once, you know.

J.M.:   Yeah, that often happens. But I think he'll win this time.

Patricia: It sounds like it's a pretty close race.

J.M.:   Yeah, it does. That's another reason I want to help. Besides, with Eastern Europe falling apart and freedom breaking out everywhere, it's an exciting time to be involved in politics. You don't get involved, Trisha?

Patricia: I pose for the official family pictures—but that's it. My dad and I don't get along very well. And I think if people knew him as well as I do, they wouldn't vote for him.

J.M.: That's too bad you feel that way. Uncle Franklin could be a state senator some day. He's a good man.

Patricia: *(a touch of bitterness)* Yeah, well, I've listened to so much politics at home that I could choke. I'm tempted to go get pregnant so I could have an abortion just to shut them up. Funny thing is, my dad complains all the time about how his dad forced him to be a conscientious objector during Vietnam—and he spouts off about how he decided *then* he'll never let himself be forced to live out someone else's beliefs again—even though he met Mom when he went to Colorado in 1-W! *Now* he tries to force me to believe like he believes. He's just as bad as he says Grandpa was.

J.M.: Whoa! You do seem upset. Sounds like your last year in high school is driving you up the wall!

Patricia: I can't wait to leave home.

J.M.: I know how you feel. I felt the same way. Can you imagine being the son of a college professor whose latest book is titled, *God Died Among the Mennonites*?!

Patricia: I liked it. I think your dad's a sensational writer.

J.M.: I agree with the sensational part.

Patricia: I meant, I think he's very talented. I'm very proud of my Uncle Jake.

J.M.: *(going to the window to look out)* Yeah, well, you don't know what it's like to have divorced parents. Sometimes I feel like an orphan. The shadow of my little sister's death never really went away.

Patricia: I'm sorry for you, J.M.

J.M.: Although, I must say, I'm as surprised as anybody that my parents are seeing each other again.

Patricia: I heard they were.

J.M.: Yeah, Dad persuaded my mom to come along today. She's on the walk with the rest of them.

Patricia: Oh, that's nice. That makes me feel really good.

J.M.: Hey, I heard you're applying to Harvard.

Patricia: Yeah. But that's no big deal. Being *accepted* would be a big deal.

J.M.: Oh, you're a good student, aren't you?

Patricia: I suppose. But you know my dad won't let me go to Harvard. Can you imagine!—Franklin Zimmerman's daughter at that liberal, stuck-up Harvard! Never. What he'd like is to be able to tell people that I was *accepted* at Harvard, but then have me go to a place like Liberty.

J.M.: Liberty's not so bad.

Patricia: Oh, yeah? How come you didn't go there? *(sees Joe enter)* Oh, hi, Joe. *(Joe is 19, a farmer, dressed in a plain shirt, a sweater, and slacks appropriate for the group he belongs to. He is less reserved than Mervin, but clearly a bit shy around his "worldly" cousins.)*

Joe: Hello, Patricia. J.M. *(He nods, but keeps his distance.)*

J.M.: Hi, Joe. What's new? *(They remain seated, he remains standing.)*

Joe: Not much.

Patricia: Nice day for a walk.

Joe: It's a beautiful day. The men took a shortcut back and are out looking around the barn. *(awkward silence)*

J.M.: We were just discussing colleges. I guess you aren't going to college, are you, Joe?

Joe: I plan to farm.

J.M.: Helping your dad?

Patricia: Oh, J.M., hadn't you heard that Joe is moving here to farm the homeplace?

J.M.: Really? No, I didn't know. Where will you live?

Joe: Here.

J.M.: Here? In this house?

Joe: Grandma is moving into the two rooms on the west end of the house, and Emma and I will live in this part.

J.M.:   Emma?

Patricia: He's getting married. Don't your parents tell you anything, J.M.?!

J.M.:   Sorry. *(stands)* Congratulations. *(crosses to shake his hand)* So, who is this hot little number? I know her?

Joe: I beg your pardon?

J.M.:   Who is this Emma?

Joe: I don't appreciate people talking about my wife-to-be that way.

J.M.:   Sorry. *(He raises his hands in apology, then crosses to another part of the room to diffuse the situation.)*

Patricia: She is a nice young woman. I met her here at Grandma's one evening this summer. *(Again, an awkward silence.)*

Joe: I think I'll see where the men are. *(He turns and exits abruptly upstage right.)*

J.M.:   Wow—I had no idea.

Patricia: *(giggling)* I shouldn't say this—but aren't Uncle Mervin and Aunt Velma's kids—*(giggles)*—a bunch of gekes! *(can hardly control her laughter, partly caused by the humor of the idea, and partly by her embarrassment.)* I could never live like them—they're so narrow!

J.M.:   Oh, really, Trisha—you can be so cruel. *(Then he, too, starts to laugh, and soon the two of them are feeding off each other's laughter. When the cycle of hilarity has begun to fade, Franklin strides in. His suit speaks "wealth, conservative, and proper." He is now 40 years old.)*

Franklin: Oh, you made it, Trisha.

Patricia: Yes, I did, Dad. And believe it or not, I brought Grandma a pie from the restaurant for our supper.

Franklin: Good. Well, I'm going to skip over to the dedication at the park for an hour or so, and then I'll be back.

Patricia: *(needling)* Working on Sunday again, Dad?

J.M.: May I ride along, Uncle Franklin?

Franklin: Oh, if you wish. I could use someone to help hand out literature.

J.M.: Good. I'll come along. *(gets ready to go)*

Franklin: Okay, J.M. I appreciate young people who believe in something. Trisha, tell Grandma where I went.

Patricia: Tell her yourself. I'm not doing your dirty work.

J.M.: I'll tell her.

Franklin: Oh, never mind, she probably won't miss us. Let's go. *(J.M. follows him out as Patricia watches after them. Then she walks slowly back to her chair and picks up the photo album. She is barely seated when Jake, Mervin, and Joe come in. Mervin wears a plain suit, Jake a tie and sports jacket with a college look.)*

Jake: Well, that's really impressive, Joe. It sounds like you will get this place back to where it was before Grandpa died.

Joe: I'll do my best.

Mervin: I could use a drink of water. *(moves toward kitchen)* Joe, we'll have to head home soon to milk the cows.

Joe: I'm ready when you are.

Mervin: Oh, hello, Patricia, I didn't see you sitting there. *(He crosses to shake her hand.)* Missed you at noon.

Patricia: Yeah, I'm sorry I couldn't make it, Uncle Mervin.

Mervin: Well, it's nice you could come for part of it. Unfortunately we'll have to head home soon to do the milking. But we hope to come back later. Aunt Velma can stay, though.

Patricia: I understand.

Mervin: What happened to your father? I thought I saw him come in here a few minutes ago.

Patricia: *(caught between covering for her dad and exposing him)* He—uh—he said he'll be back in about an hour.

Mervin: Politics?

Patricia: Don't blame me, Uncle Mervin.

Mervin: *(cautious to criticize his brother in front of his brother's daughter)* Oh, well, I suppose he believes in what he's doing.

Patricia: He gets an A+ on that score!

Mervin: *(looks at her for a moment, then decides the subject's had enough discussion)* Well, I'm going to get that drink. You thirsty, Joe?

Joe: Yes, I am, Pop. *(They both exit to the kitchen.)*

Patricia: *(standing up, her body language adjusting)* Hello, Uncle Jake.

Jake: Hello, Trisha. How are you today? *(Each clearly has affection for the other.)*

Patricia: Good. *(pause)* I've been meaning to tell you how much I'm enjoying your Saturday morning class at the college.

Jake: I'm glad to hear that. I feel privileged to have you in the class.

Patricia: I think it's neat that you let some high school seniors join the course.

Jake: You're a good writer, Trisha. I thought your poetry was especially strong.

Patricia: (glowing) Thanks, Uncle Jake. I don't think I got to tell you how much I liked your new novel.

Jake: Thanks. (clearly pleased) That means a lot, coming from someone like you—a relative, you know.

Patricia: I loved the title—*God Died Among the Mennonites*—I thought it was sensational! *(pause)* May I ask you something confidential sometime?

Jake: *(looking around)* Sure. Anytime.

Patricia: Maybe after class next week?

Jake: That doesn't suit too well, but—well, what's wrong with now?

Patricia: Okay. You know, you gave us that big writing assignment related to our identity—and I've been digging into my past—I interviewed Mother's parents when they were here from Colorado over Christmas—and I hope to interview Grandma Zimmerman sometime—maybe even tonight yet.

Jake: Okay—that's confidential?

Patricia: No. *(glances around nervously)* In my research in our attic at home, I discovered these old diaries of Mother's— before she was married—I mean, they're locked in a box at the bottom of a deep drawer—but I managed to open it—*(laughs sheepishly)* and I discovered a secret about Mother that I'm not sure my dad knows.

Jake: Well, well. Old boyfriends?

Patricia: *(glancing around to make sure no one is hearing)* Oh, no, much worse than that.

Jake: Worse?

Patricia: It could ruin Dad's election possibilities. *(Jake waits as Patricia glances around)* I discovered my mother had an abortion before she was married to my dad.

Jake: *(lowered voice)* You're kidding!

Patricia: No, I certainly am not.

Jake: Isn't that an irony!

Patricia: *(glancing around)* I mean, do you know anyone in Lancaster County more vocal against abortion than my parents—they march, they speak, they're on radio and TV—

Jake: Sounds like Jennie and me twenty years ago!

Patricia: So here's my question. I know this guy Robert who works for the newspaper—do you think I should give him the diaries?

Jake: You mean, to publish?

Patricia: The public has a right to know, don't you think?

Jake: *(low, but intense)* But you could ruin his election!

Patricia: A *hypocrite should* be exposed if—*(Suddenly Mervin and Joe re-enter from the kitchen, and from upstage right, everyone comes pouring in from the walk: Rhoda, followed by Jennie, Susan, Shirley, and Velma and her two younger children, Junior and Anna Mary. It seems as though they are all talking at once.)*

Susan: *(walking toward Patricia)* Well, Patricia, you made it.
            *(Patricia pulls out of her conversation with Jake and
            goes to shake her grandmother's hand.)*

Patricia: Yes, thank you, Grandma. I'm glad to be here.

Shirley: We just had the nicest walk, honey.

Patricia: Sorry I missed it. *(Jennie, Rhoda, and Velma have all
            found seats.)* Hello, Aunt Jennie. It's nice you could
            come.

Jennie: Thanks. I'm enjoying it.

Mervin: *(to Susan)* Mother, Joe and I are taking Junior here and
            we're heading home to do the milking. We'll be back as
            soon as we can, but don't wait to eat until we get back.

Susan: You'd like us to wait?

Mervin: No, I said—don't wait. We'll grab a little something
            when we get back.

Susan: Well, I think we can all wait. We're in no rush.

Rhoda: I'm still stuffed from that big Sunday dinner.

Shirley: It was really good, Mother dear.

Mervin: Well, we're off then. See you later.

Velma: Junior, you know where your barn clothes are. *(He nods.)*

Susan: Bye now. *(The three of them exit upstage right. Anna Mary exits to the kitchen. Jake appears to drift toward the doorway to go out on the porch. Velma's question stops him.)*

Velma: Jake, I saw the article in the paper about your new book.

Jake: Oh, you did?

Jennie: It was a nice article, I thought.

Velma: I haven't seen the book itself—but I was wondering about its title—could you explain it to me?

Jake: It makes more sense if you read it.

Velma: Well, I'm sure of that. But since I haven't, does it refer to the past or the future?

Jake: I'm not sure I follow.

Rhoda: I think she means about God dying.

Velma: Exactly. Is God already dead, in your opinion, or is he about to die—among the Mennonites?

Patricia: *(to Jake's defense)* I think Uncle Jake has written a wonderful book, Aunt Velma, and I'd encourage you to read it.

Shirley: Trisha, please don't interfere.

Velma: Mervin thinks you're ripping off the Mennonites. Because who besides Mennonites would buy a book with a sensational title like that?

Jennie: Mervin was just here.

Jake: Yeah, he didn't say a word about it to me.

Velma: He wouldn't say it to your face. But I wanted you to
          know not all Mennonites appreciate being smeared that
          way in the newspaper. Where do you go to church,
          Jake—if you go?

Jake: I—ah—we attend the Presbyterian church there on the
          edge of campus, sometimes. It's just a block away.

Velma: How long is it, Jake, since you've regularly attended a
          Mennonite church?

Jake: Regularly? Not since Annie's death more than ten years
          ago.

Susan: Maybe we should change the subject. *(She carries paper
          cups around to each person and pours lemonade from a
          pitcher in her hand.)*

Shirley: Where does it say in the Bible that you have to be a
          Mennonite to be a Christian? I married Franklin
          because when we met at Youth for Christ there near my
          home in Colorado, he was a really terrific Christian. I
          didn't care a thing about being a Mennonite.

Velma: Oh, that's right, you folks are going to Red Rose
          Independent Church, aren't you? One more who's left
          the Mennonites.

Shirley: We feel more comfortable there. *(She throws a warning
          glance at her daughter, but unsuccessfully.)*

Patricia: Speak for yourself, Mom.

Susan: I do think we could change the subject. How about a game of Probe or Aggravation?

Jennie: Velma, I hear your brother and you are having problems at your church.

Velma: *(surprised)* Where'd you hear that?

Jennie: Is it true?

Velma: *(uncomfortable)* I guess, sorta.

Jennie: *(partly sarcastic)* So even in your pure spotless world of right and wrong, there's a lack of unity and peace?

Velma: *(clearly hurt)* You could say that. I'm sorry if you think I act like we don't have problems.

Rhoda: We all have problems, don't we, Jennie?

Jennie: It's just that Velma seems free to criticize everyone—I thought maybe she should be honest about her own world.

Velma: My brother and his family think our church is too lenient—so they've helped to start a more conservative group—*(her voice almost breaks)*. A lot of our best friends went along—even some of our best young people left. Emma's parents went along to the new group.

Patricia: Joe's fiance?

Velma: *(sober, quiet)* Yeah, Joe and Emma say they're staying with us. But I know they're really struggling. It's a very hard thing for Emma to go against her parents.

Susan: Oh, my. I didn't know about her parents.

Velma: We need the grace of God as much as anybody, Jennie.

Rhoda: Sounds like the church I just left.

Jake: Rhoda, you don't have to go into it.

Rhoda: Well the truth is, a lot of us in this family disapprove of the way the rest of us express our faith. And yet we all end up with imperfect church situations.

Patricia: *(enthusiastically)* Did any of you hear Aunt Rhoda preach during her three years as pastor at the church out in Indiana?

Rhoda: Assistant pastor.

Patricia: She was good. I heard her twice, and I wish Dr. Williams at our church could speak that well.

Rhoda: Thanks, Trisha. I only wish a few more at First Mennonite had agreed with you.

Velma: *(catching on)* Oh, I'm not up on this.

Rhoda: Velma, I know you're going to say "I told you so."

Velma: *(abrupt)* You were fired?

Rhoda: *(laughing in spite of herself)* To put it bluntly, yes.

Velma: *(with real feeling)* Oh, you poor thing.

Jennie: Did they eliminate the whole position?

Rhoda: No, they said they didn't want to have a woman pastor after all, so they replaced me with a young man fresh out of seminary.

Jennie: Wow! Talk about discrimination.

Jake: That's rough. I'm sorry, Rhoda.

Shirley: Maybe it's all for the best. *(She clearly thinks so. Rhoda makes a face at her.)*

Velma: *(laughing)* Oh, Rhoda, when you made that face, you reminded me of that time when we were still teenagers and we went to this cabin north of Williamsport.

Rhoda: *(starts to laugh)* You mean the one where the door wouldn't stay shut?

Velma: Yeah, wasn't that the funniest thing! *(laughing, standing to demonstrate)* Rhoda was scared that the guys in the next cabin might wander in if the door wasn't latched— so she insisted on sleeping in this stupid, slouchy chair against the door. *(demonstrates)* It was the funniest looking thing! *(laughs heartily)*

Rhoda: *(laughing)* Oh, we had so much fun in those days! *(Everyone is smiling, warmed by the story.)*

Velma: Yeah, we sure did!

Rhoda: *(her comment just sort of slips out, unguarded)* What happened to us?

Velma: *(with a touch of sadness)* We got older. We grew apart. More than we should have probably. *(It's a very special moment, and everyone senses it.)*

Susan: I can use a few hands in the kitchen. *(Everyone starts to get up.)*

Shirley: But I'm still stuffed from that big Sunday dinner.

Susan: We can at least start cutting up the vegetables.

Rhoda: You know, Velma, I hadn't thought about that Williamsport trip for a long time. *(By now, most of them have gone to the kitchen. Patricia lingers, as does Jake.)*

Velma: *(as she disappears to the kitchen)* Me either.

Jake: *(after everyone else has disappeared)* You have a minute, Trisha?

Patricia: Sure, Uncle Jake. It's great to see you and Jennie back together.

Jake: Thanks. *(pause)* About the matter we were discussing earlier—

Patricia: *(nods, voice lowered)* The diaries?

Jake: *(carefully)* Yeah, I'm not sure what to say. I guess I'd be pretty cautious on it if I were you.

Patricia: You mean don't publish it? Uncle Jake, I thought you would cheer me on.

Jake: Tell me the truth, Trisha—are you interested in the public's right to know—or do you want to hurt your dad? (pause) When you want to hurt someone, Trisha, you should always ask yourself what your actions will do to you, personally. Often you hurt yourself more than anyone—because you must live with yourself the rest of your life. You might destroy your dad—but can *you* just forget it and go on? I'm not sure.

Patricia: I'm surprised by your response. Maybe it's something I'm willing to risk.

Jake: Think about it.

Patricia: *(slightly insulted)* I'm not a baby anymore, you know.

Jake: Oh, I'm quite aware of that. I didn't mean to upset you.

Patricia: *(snapping)* Well, you did. I finally have a chance to get even with my dad—and you're telling me to drop it.

Jake: I'm not telling you what to do. I simply gave you my opinion. Part of me would like to put Franklin Zimmerman in his place, too. But I'm more concerned about your future than his. Revenge has a way of coming home to roost.

Patricia: The voice of experience?

Jake: Regrettably, yes.

Patricia: *(after a pause)* I'll think about it.

Jake: Good. *(Jennie enters suddenly from the kitchen; she clearly has something on her mind but her carriage does not portend a crisis.)*

Jennie: Jake, I think I'll be taking off.

Jake: So soon? What happened?

Jennie: I told you I might not stay the whole day.

Patricia: *(going to exit downstage right)* Excuse me.

Jennie: Oh, no, Trisha, please don't let me break up your conversation. Jake, you can call me later. *(Patricia hesitates.)*

Jake: *(not happy)* Jennie, I wish you'd stay.

Jennie: Jake, you promised me space. I'm not mad. I simply told your mother I had other plans.

Jake: Do you?

Jennie: I do now.

Jake: *(clearly upset)* Why are you hurting me in front of my family?

Jennie: I'm not hurting anyone, Jake. Just ease up. This'll never work if you crowd me.

Jake: Okay, okay. I'm sorry. I'll call you later.

Jennie: Thanks. *(pausing)* You know, I forgot how much like you all of them are. *(moves to go)* Nice to see you again, Trisha.

Patricia: Yeah, you, too, Aunt Jennie. *(Jennie goes out.)* I'm sorry, Uncle Jake. I tried to leave.

Jake: *(not fully recovered)* What did she mean, how much they remind her of me? I'm not like my family, really. Am I? I always thought I was the one who broke free.

Patricia: Oh, yes, Uncle Jake. I've always admired you for that. *(He just stares at her.)* Well, maybe I better help in the kitchen. *(He remains silent while she crosses to the kitchen. She pauses before going out.)* Thanks for the conversation, Uncle Jake.

Jake: *(still lost in thought)* Sure, Trisha. Any time. *(She goes out as he stares into space, lost in thought, then turns to look toward the spot where Jennie disappeared. Lights come down. Music bridges to the next scene.)*

ACT THREE, Scene Two

Same set. Later that afternoon.

Rhoda is standing on stage apron downstage right as spot comes up on her She seems sad, unhappy. The main set is half-lit to give the feeling of late afternoon. A second spot comes up on stage apron downstage left. Susan enters this spot and immediately sees Rhoda.

Susan: Something wrong?

Rhoda: *(surprised)* Oh, Mother—no, not really.

Susan: Something someone said?

Rhoda: No—not really.

Susan: Okay—I'll leave you alone. *(She turns to go.)*

Rhoda: It was nice what Velma said.

Susan: *(turning back)* Yes, I thought so.

Rhoda: It's easy to forget how good a person she is.

Susan: She and Mervin have really stuck by me.

Rhoda: I know she thinks it's outrageous for women to be
         pastors—but I must say I felt more caring empathy from
         her this afternoon—about what happened to me—than I
         have from almost anyone.

Susan: She's always been that way. She knows what she believes—but she really cares about other people as persons. *(pause)* The two of you are very similar in that way, you know.

Rhoda: Oh, I'm not that sure about myself.

Susan: You've been through a hard thing.

Rhoda: Sometimes I feel so alone. As we talked this afternoon, I suddenly remembered what it was like to be young— all the dreams we had. Then I looked at my brothers— married, with families. They're all settled down and know what they want. Jake and Jennie are even getting back together.

Susan: It feels like an answer to prayer.

Rhoda: But I'm alone. And furthermore, they've all left the church. I'm the only one in the Mennonite church anymore.

Susan: Mervin and Velma are Mennonites.

Rhoda: You know what I mean, Mother. I'm the only one who stuck by the church I was brought up in—and I'm not sure why. There doesn't seem to be a place for me.

Susan: Oh, Rhoda, don't say that. You've done so much for the church. People just forget to express their appreciation.

Rhoda: Sometimes I think it's the weak ones who stay—those of us who don't have enough backbone to strike out on our own.

Susan: You really think that you and I are a bunch of boring, spineless weaklings?

Rhoda: *(laughs gently)* No, I guess we're not, are we?

Susan: *(after a bit)* I should be getting back to the house.

Rhoda: That's fine. Thanks for listening. I think maybe I'll take a walk through the meadow. I'll be back a bit later.

Susan: Take your time, Rhoda. You don't need to apologize. Remember, we all love you. You're the only Rhoda we have.

Rhoda: *(touched)* Thanks, Mother. *(Susan smiles and exits spot to left. Lights come down as Rhoda looks after her, then exits stage right. Music bridges the scene—a very short bridge.)*

ACT THREE, Scene Three

Same set. Later that day.

Franklin and Jake are on their feet in the middle of a heated exchange. Supper is over and they are alone.

Jake: *(trying not to lose control)* Hey, Frank, I don't want to take this any further. I really should be going.

Franklin: He finally gets cornered, and now he wants to run!

Jake: Cornered?! You're just so stubborn you won't admit the truth.

Franklin: Why do you think democracy is suddenly breaking out all over the world, Dr. Professor? Because Reagan was tough. He made those communists spend all their money on weapons and now they're so poor that the people are rebelling and throwing them out. It was one of the greatest battles for freedom in the history of the world— and Reagan never dropped a bomb! A peaceful war. You should love that, Jake—you've always been for peace!

Jake: If you think Ronald Reagan had a single idea about what was going on elsewhere in the world during those eight sleepwalking years, you're as unintelligent as he was!

Franklin: You're calling me stupid?!

Jake: *(alarmed)* Whoa—let's stop right there. I quit.

Franklin: *(laughing sarcastically)* You always were a quitter. You'd rather go home and write some outrageous book for your students to faint over—rather than admit you're wrong.

Jake: Okay, I'm wrong.

Franklin: You are?

Jake: Isn't that what you want to hear?

Franklin: You're mocking me, aren't you? Well, you can look down on me, brother, from your ivory tower—you can mock me—but "God is not mocked."

Jake: Is that original with you?

Franklin: *(angry)* Whatever happened to you, Jake? Where has all your sarcasm gotten you? Sometimes I don't even know if you're saved, if you're a believer anymore.

Jake: *(miffed)* I can tell you this, Frank. I'd rather that my son were an unbeliever than a pompous Fundamentalist like you!

Franklin: *(smiling victoriously)* Well, isn't that interesting! I suppose that's why J.M. wants to help me in my campaign!

Jake: *(without a beat)* And I suppose that's why your daughter's running to me for advice! *(For a moment they both fall silent, frozen in angry combat, then drained and weary from the battle. Shirley enters from the kitchen to check on the commotion.)*

Shirley: Sounds pretty loud in here.

Franklin: *(to Shirley)* Sorry.

Shirley: We should go, Franklin, honey. Everyone else is gone. *(Susan enters from the kitchen.)*

Jake: I should go, too.

Susan: Thanks for coming.

Shirley: I guess we drove in two cars, Franklin. You coming?

Franklin: In a minute.

Jake: See you guys. *(pause)* Franklin, we'll have to keep talking.

Franklin: It seems like we can't help it. *(Franklin and Jake both chuckle.)*

Jake: *(as he goes out)* Good-bye, now. Thanks, Mom. *(Jake exits.)*

Shirley: I'll see you soon, Franklin. Good-bye, Mother dear.

Susan: Good-bye, Shirley. *(Shirley goes out. Susan sighs, smiles, and starts to straighten the tablecloth. She glances at Franklin who stands, watching her)*

Franklin: *(warmly)* Big day?

Susan: Yes—but an enjoyable one. *(She goes to sit in her favorite chair)*

Franklin: I wanted to say I was sorry I slipped out this afternoon without telling you.

Susan: Shirley explained.

Franklin: She did? I'm sorry if it upset you.

Susan: If I let everything upset me that my children do with which I disagree—I'd be in bad shape.

Franklin: But why must you disagree with what I'm doing?

Susan: I don't want to argue with you, Franklin. I thought maybe you'd had enough arguing for one day—I could hear you and Jake going at it a few minutes ago.

Franklin: *(offhand, but with purpose)* Well, I hope I can at least count on your vote on election day.

Susan: I'm afraid you're asking for something I can't give.

Franklin: It's going to be really embarrassing to me, Mother, if I can't know that you voted—for *me*.

Susan: You know that I don't vote, Franklin. Never have, never will. It's against my principles. Your father felt the same, you know that. We don't want to get mixed up with politics and government.

Franklin: But, Mother, I thought you could make an exception for me.

Susan: Where will it end? Jennie was just saying this afternoon that she's planning to run for the school board.

Franklin: She is? Oh, wow, what a disaster!

Susan: You think I should vote for her?

Franklin: Absolutely not! She's so liberal it's scary.

Susan: See what I mean?

Franklin: What?

Susan: I'm better off sticking to my convictions. *(Franklin gets up, sighs a heavy sigh, and begins to walk away. His mother looks after him.)* You worried?

Franklin: How do you mean?

Susan: Afraid you'll lose?

Franklin: *(firm)* I *must* win.

Susan: You must?

Franklin: *(walking back a bit)* I don't want to lose again. *(pause)* You take Jake—the newspapers treat him like an important person. And I suppose he is. But me—ever since that last election they treat me like yesterday's leftovers. No matter that I've been a successful realtor— and that we have a growing Christian bookstore.

Susan: *(calmly)* I wouldn't live my life to please the newspapers.

Franklin: I think you know what I mean, Mother. Don't you see?

Susan: You should learn to relax more, Franklin. Maybe you and Jake both worry about the newspapers too much.

(Patricia enters upstage right, followed by J.M. who has two cameras swinging from his neck.)

Patricia: Oh, you're still here, Dad?

Franklin: I was just leaving.

Susan: So you came back? *(gets to her feet)*

Patricia: Grandma, it's up to you. J.M. said he could shoot some pictures of you as we talk—which I'd really appreciate since he has to head back to college this evening yet. But if you're too tired, I'll come another time.

Susan: Oh, no, now's okay, I guess. If it gets too long, I'll tell you.

Franklin: What's happening?

Patricia: I'm doing a paper for my writing class about my family background. And J.M.'s taking some photos.

Franklin: Oh.

Patricia: The sooner you leave, the sooner we can start.

Franklin: Nothing like being pushed out! I didn't know you were a photographer, J.M.

J.M.: Oh, a little.

Franklin: *(comes to shake her hand)* Good-bye, Mother. Thanks for everything.

Susan: Sure. It's always good to have the family home.

Franklin: *(turning to go)* Good night.

J.M.: See you, Uncle Franklin.

Patricia: Bye, Dad. *(Franklin goes out.)*

Susan: So, I guess I should be a little nervous.

Patricia: Oh, no, just sit wherever you want, and I'll ask a few questions. Don't mind J.M.

Susan: I guess it'll flash a lot.

J.M.: No, I shoot with available light. It has more feeling.

Susan: Available light? *(chuckles)* Sounds a bit like life. *(She sits, Patricia perches half-seated on a chair nearby, and J.M. crouches as he begins to shoot. Susan tries to act unaffected by the attention.)*

Patricia: *(without a beat)* So, I guess I'll start in. Please don't let my questions offend you or startle you.

Susan: I don't think I could be too thin-skinned, Patricia, and go through everything I've been through. Just ask what you want.

Patricia: Okay. Would you say you have reached your life's aspirations?

Susan: Aspirations?

Patricia: Yeah, you know, what things did you aspire to be when you were young?

Susan: *(taken aback)* Oh, I don't know that we had anything you
           could call aspirations. *(pause)* We just wanted to farm—
           and to follow God.

*(Patricia looks up, startled, and J.M. looks up from his camera.
They are frozen for a moment. The lights come down.)*

End of play.

About the Author

Merle Good has authored numerous plays and books. His first novel, *Happy as the Grass Was Green,* was produced as the movie *Hazel's People,* starring Geraldine Page and Pat Hingle.

Good and his wife Phyllis live in Lancaster, PA, with their two daughters.